Coordinating Multijurisdiction Litigation

Litigation

A Pocket Guide for Judges

Federal Judicial Center

National Center for State Courts

United States Judicial Panel on Multidistrict Litigation

2013

This resource was created in furtherance of the Federal Judicial Center's statutory mission to develop educational materials for the judicial branch. While the Center regards the content as responsible and valuable it does not reflect policy or recommendations of the Board of the Federal Judicial Center or any other agency or organization.

Contents

Introduction

Multijurisdiction litigation poses numerous challenges to the state and federal courts. With mutual respect and two-way communication, however, these challenges can be overcome. There is and should be respect among judges, as well as respect for principles of federalism, both of which foster cooperation to advance multijurisdiction litigation. To cooperate effectively, both state and federal judges must understand the problems facing the judiciary today, including budget constraints, docket congestion, and staffing limitations. By achieving such an understanding, judges in both systems will be in a position to develop the joint communication and cooperation necessary to manage some of the most challenging cases.

> *The key to successful communication is as simple as mutual respect.*

The suggestions and recommendations in this guide resulted from an unprecedented collaboration of ten veteran federal and state judges. Their decades of experience in managing complex, multijurisdiction litigation provide valuable lessons in the art of judicial cooperation, as described below.

This guide is not intended as a comprehensive treatment of this important topic, but rather as a brief overview and a prompt to begin communication. There are a number of excellent resources on this topic, including the Federal Judicial Center's *Manual for Complex Litigation, Fourth*, and the National Center for State Courts' 2006 commentary on the *Manual* for state judges. These resources and many others are listed in the Appendix. Each section below also includes suggested readings.

Advantages of Coordination

Multijurisdiction litigation is a relatively common occurrence in the modern legal world. The phrase evokes images of mass tort litigation—thousands of cases against a limited number of defendants, most perhaps consolidated in a federal multidistrict litigation (MDL) proceeding but with many other cases in numerous state courts. However, multijurisdiction litigation is a much broader phenomenon. There are multijurisdiction disputes involving just one case in state court and a related case in federal court—commercial matters, insurance coverage disputes, even securities cases can span the jurisdictional divide.

Coordination can help judges address many of the challenges created by multijurisdiction litigation. Obviously, litigating similar cases in multiple jurisdictions can strain the resources of the parties and result in unnecessary duplication of effort and considerable inefficiencies. Moreover, the decisions or actions of a single court can significantly affect cases pending in other jurisdictions, sometimes to the detriment of the parties' interests and the fairness of the overall resolution. For example, when one judge schedules a trial, witnesses involved will be unavailable for deposition or trial in another court during that time. Duplicate attorney attachment for trial is another potential pitfall.

Judges should not surrender their responsibility to manage their own cases and their responsibility to apply the law of their jurisdictions to legal issues. However, it is wise for judges to consider the impact of their decisions on the broader litigation. Every judge involved in the broader litigation will want the other judges to consider how their decisions impact his or her cases, which is why communication is important. In the end, it is a matter of mutual respect and comity.

Multijurisdiction litigation can involve just one state case and a related federal case.

Knowing what is going on in the entire litigation also protects a judge from issuing rulings that inadvertently provide one set of attorneys with a strategic advantage. Again, the key to preventing this kind of gamesmanship is not managing one's own cases in the dark.

It is important for judges in all jurisdictions to be attentive to the issues raised by multijurisdiction litigation, regardless of the scale of the litigation. Judges should make it a practice to require parties to identify related cases in other jurisdictions, at least when there is some reason to suspect that such cases exist. When appropriate, coordination of schedules and discovery among multiple jurisdictions may create efficiencies, allow for a more rational allocation of judicial resources, and eliminate unnecessary duplication. Coordination also promotes and permits constructive collaboration, not only by the judges, but also by counsel working with the judges presiding in the various jurisdictions. In the end, it may also promote a more optimal outcome for the parties than would have resulted from a piecemeal approach.

There may, of course, be impediments to successful coordination. Differences in the laws of multiple jurisdictions can create difficulties. Disputes among the attorneys involved are likely to arise—especially over compensation for their work. Not every judge will be comfortable discussing case management with other judges, even if the discussion is limited to scheduling. All of these topics will be addressed in this pocket guide.

Communication

Of course, the first task—the *best* way to know about the progress of the multijurisdiction litigation as a whole—is to *communicate*. Below are four suggested steps to initiate coordination in multijurisdiction litigation:

Step 1: Identify related cases

Identify related cases as a part of early case management. In states in which Federal Rule of Civil Procedure 16(b)-type scheduling conferences are not regularly held, it may be wise to hold one when you suspect that there are related cases in other jurisdictions. In your initial order scheduling the conference, notify the attorneys that they should be prepared to discuss related cases and hold them to it. Direct the parties—particularly the defendant(s)—to identify all related cases in other jurisdictions. Let the attorneys know that once they identify the related cases, you will consider communicating with the judges in those cases and you would prefer to have the attorneys' agreement to do so.

Step 2: Initiate communication

When you have identified the related cases and the judges in the other jurisdictions, and after notice to counsel of your intent to communicate with those judges, initiate communication. Introduce yourself and ask the other judge(s) if coordination will be useful.

It may be obvious, but a key to initiating a successful communication is mutual respect. Do not expect judges in other jurisdictions to alter the schedules of their cases to accommodate your schedule. But you should be open to coordinating schedules to avoid duplication and inefficiencies, when possible.

In some cases, judges in other jurisdictions may be reluctant to discuss coordination because of ethical concerns, especially concern about the potential for *ex parte* communications. However, judicial codes of conduct generally allow judges to coordinate with other judges or even encourage judges to cooperate with other judges in the administration of court business.

If you receive a phone call from a judge in another jurisdiction and have some reservations about the communication, tell the judge that you want to notify attorneys in your cases of the communication. Inform your attorneys that you intend to communicate with the judge. It works best to obtain the attorneys' cooperation at the outset—on the record, if possible. As will be discussed, attorneys may be reluctant to coordinate across jurisdictional lines. Be clear—let the attorneys know that you will be in communication with judges in other jurisdictions. Outline how contact will be made and what subjects will be covered. To the extent practicable, give the attorneys an opportunity to have input into the process and to voice any concerns they may have. Then, return the phone call.

> *Transparency: Letting the attorneys know, as early as possible, that you are communicating with other judges can head off later charges of interference.*

Or, if you have spoken with a judge from another jurisdiction, inform the attorneys at the next available opportunity that you have communicated, and describe generally the information that was exchanged. Either approach may be acceptable, depending on your local rules and practices.

Step 3: Address preliminary issues

The initial conversations should include discussion of:

- the number of existing cases and potential claims in each jurisdiction;
- the status or progress of cases in each jurisdiction;

- any existing deadlines in each jurisdiction;
- the resources available in each jurisdiction for managing the litigation;
- any differences between the laws of the involved jurisdictions that could create issues in the litigation (e.g., different discovery rules, common benefit fund issues); and
- "ground rules" for further communication and coordination, including the best means for maintaining the communication.

Step 4: Maintain communication

Depending on the nature of the litigation, consider appointing liaison counsel or a liaison committee to help you and the other judges keep in contact.

From the outset, and on an ongoing basis: Show the attorneys how state and federal judges can work together.

The remainder of this guide addresses specific opportunities for coordination, as well as issues you are likely to encounter in your efforts to coordinate.

Suggested readings

Paula L. Hannaford-Agor, Comment: Federal MCL Fourth and Suggestions for State Court Management of Mass Litigation (National Center for State Courts 2006)

Francis E. McGovern, *Rethinking Cooperation Among Judges in Mass Tort Litigation*, 44 UCLA L. Rev. 1851 (1997)

Francis E. McGovern, *Toward a Cooperative Strategy for Federal and State Judges in Mass Torts Litigation*, 148 Penn. L. Rev. 1867 (2000)

Gregory E. Mize & James Fletcher, Judicial Ethics Considerations When Managing Multi-jurisdiction Litigation (National Center for State Courts 2012)

Federal Judicial Center, Manual for Complex Litigation, Fourth (2004), § 20.3

Technology

Because cooperation is primarily about communicating, technology can be enormously beneficial in multijurisdiction litigation by making information exchange easy and allowing people who are far apart to work together. Below are some technology-based tools for enhancing cooperation.

- *Listserv*—A listserv is a list of email addresses, centrally maintained. If someone sends an email to the listserv, the email will go to every email address on the list, even if the sender does not know those addresses. Through a listserv, judges with related litigation can keep in touch and circulate key documents, such as scheduling orders, in their cases.

- *Audio and video conferencing*—High quality video conferencing is second only to travel in its ability to bring people around the same—here virtual—table. Cost typically is the only downside. Web-based services may be less expensive than stand-alone video conferencing systems. For hearings and "science day" presentations, video may be worth the cost. In other situations, audio is often perfectly adequate, and it is simpler and cheaper. For conference calls, it may be wise to choose a format in which the caller pays, not the organizer.

- *E-service providers*—These services can make the dockets of multiple cases available on one website to all parties and judges. Jurisdictional differences may affect the feasibility of this feature; some jurisdictions require using certain providers, while others forbid a judge from naming any particular provider.

- *Litigation website*—A court may create, or direct the parties to create, a website to house pretrial orders, transcripts, and other key documents. This is fairly common in large federal MDLs and in much complex state litigation. Such websites enable other courts to keep abreast of developments. E-service providers can create and support a litigation website for multiple courts.

- *Web-based calendars*—Being able to layer calendared items from multiple proceedings onto one calendar can facilitate coordination of scheduling.

Managing Attorney Disputes

Disputes among attorneys across jurisdictional lines may take many forms, but the underlying cause of many, if not most, disputes will be money. Perhaps the thorniest problem stems from a practice common in federal MDL proceedings but not in state court: the common benefit fund. Many state judges may not even be aware of this practice, and some states may not allow such a fund. Many federal judges may not be aware that the common benefit approach can create conflict with state practices. As with most case management matters, successful resolution is more likely the earlier any state-federal differences are addressed.

Under a common benefit approach, an MDL transferee judge issues an order directing that a fixed percentage (typically, though not always, 4% to 8%) of any settlement be held in a general fund to cover fees for national counsel, usually members of the plaintiff steering committee (PSC), for the additional work that they have done for the "common benefit" of parties, usually plaintiffs. Unused funds can be returned. Imposition of common benefit fees, the size of the fees, and their jurisdictional bases remain controversial but, in any case, contributions cannot be imposed by a transferee judge on attorneys who have no cases in the MDL and who do not use federal discovery material. The linkage of fees with access to discovery material is the subject of many disputes.

Disputes over common benefit fees, however difficult, have been successfully resolved by state and federal judges through communication and cooperation. There is no consensus as to the right or wrong approach to resolving these issues, but successful resolution can be achieved. Again, the importance of addressing these matters early can not be overemphasized. It is far better to have attorneys cross-notice depositions than to have attorneys fighting over access to deposition recordings or seeking duplicative depositions. These issues should be aired in the first phone call with other judges if possible.

Attorney disputes can be difficult to address effectively, and there is no "one size fits all" approach—except, that is, for early and ongoing judicial attention to potential disputes. Proactive case management may not prevent disputes, but it may help to prevent inevitable disputes from disrupting the entire litigation. A good place to start is a joint conference call with state and federal judges and lead counsel. In the Yaz litigation, for example, this approach successfully resolved discovery disputes.

It is especially important for judges presiding over MDL proceedings to open and maintain communication with state judges presiding over related cases. It is also helpful to appoint state-court liaison counsel—from among the attorneys with cases in both jurisdictions—to assist in communicating with state-court counsel.

Suggested readings

Federal Judicial Center, *Manual for Complex Litigation, Fourth* (2004), § 14.12

Barbara J. Rothstein & Catherine R. Borden, Managing Multidistrict Litigation in Products Liability Cases: A Pocket Guide for Transferee Judges (Federal Judicial Center & Judicial Panel on Multidistrict Litigation, 2011), pp. 14–16

Coordinating Discovery

A great deal has been written about coordinating discovery. Below are types of discovery that can be done jointly as well as issues that may arise in doing so.

Joint document depository
- Common benefit fund issues may arise.
- Documents/depositions should be collected/taken only once if possible, keeping in mind evidentiary differences between jurisdictions; a joint case management order may be helpful to memorialize appropriate procedures.
- A Web-based depository is more easily shared.

Coordinated scheduling of discovery deadlines
- Consider how far the litigation has developed in each jurisdiction. Later courts may be able to benefit from the work done in the earlier ones; on the other hand, sometimes a "catching up period" can allow time for mediation or early global settlement discussions. However, you will need to keep in mind what effect slowing down will have on trial dates,

settlement discussions, and completing your docket within applicable guidelines.

Shared discovery master (this was done successfully in the Avandia litigation)

- Some jurisdictions do not allow, or strongly discourage, use of special masters.
- Some judges prefer to handle discovery themselves.
- Cost is also a consideration.
- Magistrate judges, who may serve as discovery masters, are a resource for the whole court, not to be monopolized by one case.
- If there is not one shared discovery master but several different ones, discovery masters should communicate.

Uniform or joint orders, such as preservation orders, deposition protocol, plaintiff's/defendant's fact sheet or "certificate of merit" orders

- Up-front work is required for judges to agree on orders consistent with all involved jurisdictions' rules.

Cross-noticing depositions

- Ensure that all involved parties have the opportunity to ask questions (while preventing redundancy).
- If corporate depositions are conducted internationally, a special master may be appointed so that redeposition will be unnecessary. (In the Yaz litigation, a retired judge serving as special master traveled to Germany to rule on objections in global depositions.)

Encouraging shared experts

- Parties can save resources by using the same expert in multiple jurisdictions, but they may feel that using different experts will give them multiple chances to obtain a favorable result.

Designating one judge to rule on discovery objections or emergency motions

- Judges may need to alter the ruling to suit their own jurisdictions (this was done successfully in the Yaz litigation).
- The independence of the respective jurisdictions must be maintained.
- As a practical matter, the jurisdiction with the most liberal discovery rules will control.

Identifying discovery necessary for productive early settlement discussions

- The prospect of early settlement of certain issues or cases may be enhanced by early, focused discovery.
- A moratorium on plenary discovery may be advisable in some instances so that key early settlement-related discovery can be promptly completed.

"Science day" (tutorials to educate the court about the scientific issues relevant to the litigation)

- All parties must have the opportunity to contribute and attend, or ex parte concerns may arise.
- Some judges may be able to attend and sit together on the bench, some may attend by videoconference, and other judges can be given the transcript afterwards.

Daubert/Frye hearings

- This is only feasible if the judges involved are comfortable presiding together and potentially ruling differently.

In some instances, federal and state judges have held *Daubert/Frye* hearings or technical tutorials. Joint proceedings can be made to work, but keep in mind that not every judge will be comfortable with this approach. Some judges may feel that this threatens their autonomy and independence—for example, they may feel uncomfortable hearing the same testimony but reaching a different conclusion. You should respect these preferences. If judges in other jurisdictions are comfortable sitting together, be sure to work out the ground rules prior to the hearing. In both the Orthopedic Bone Screw litigation and the Avandia litigation, joint *Daubert/Frye* hearings worked well.

In your coordination efforts, remember that privilege rules vary among jurisdictions. For example, if you have ruled in favor of disclosure of materials that may be privileged in other jurisdictions, it is courteous to alert the other judges that the parties may try to introduce the material in their courts.

Suggested readings

Federal Judicial Center, Manual for Complex Litigation, Fourth (2004), § 20.313 (Pretrial discovery)

Hon. Jane R. Roth, *Coordination of Litigation in State and Federal Courts, in* Business Commercial Litigation in Federal Court 147 (Robert L. Haig, ed., 3d ed. 2011), §§ 15:21–15:27

Barbara J. Rothstein & Catherine R. Borden, Managing Multidistrict Litigation in Products Liability Cases: A Pocket Guide for Transferee Judges (Federal Judicial Center & Judicial Panel on Multidistrict Litigation, 2011), pp. 25–26, 31–36

Barbara J. Rothstein, Francis E. McGovern, & Sarah Jael Dion, *A Model Mass Tort: The PPA Experience*, 54 Drake L. Rev. 621 (2006)

Settlement

Coordination among courts is particularly beneficial as the parties approach settlement. One or more parties may even be unable or unwilling to settle your case unless the related cases are also resolved. When such a situation presents itself, codes of conduct generally prohibit judges from mediating cases in another jurisdiction without the agreement of the judges and parties in those cases. See, for example, Code of Conduct for U.S. Judges, Commentary to Canon 4A(4).

> *The parties may refuse to settle one case unless the related cases are also resolved.*

Judges differ in how actively they involve themselves in settlement negotiations. A special master may be appointed to oversee negotiations, which avoids a potential recusal if settlement does not occur. If different jurisdictions appoint the same special master, the master will be in the best position to see all the moving parts of the litigation and all the factors that influence the parties' incentives. A shared settlement special master was used in the Avandia litigation.

You may receive one or more requests to delay trial so that parties can keep working on settlement. By keeping abreast of how related cases are progressing, you will be better able to evaluate such requests.

Again, coordinate with counsel to determine if trial delays will actually thwart settlement, as firm trial dates tend to encourage resolution.

State laws may also differ on whether the court must approve a settlement, depending on the type of case and whether minors are involved.

Suggested reading

Hon. Jane R. Roth, *Coordination of Litigation in State and Federal Courts, in* Business Commercial Litigation in Federal Court 147 (Robert L. Haig, ed., 3d ed. 2011)

See generally Howard M. Erichson, *Informal Aggregation: Procedural and Ethical Implications of Coordination Among Counsel in Related Lawsuits,* 50 Duke L.J. 381 (2000)

Trial

In multijurisdiction litigation involving large numbers of cases, the first trials typically serve as bellwethers, giving parties crucial information on the value of their remaining cases and thus facilitating settlement. Judges with related cases therefore should consider coordinating selection of the first cases to go to trial. Selecting cases randomly or allowing attorneys to choose bellwethers is unlikely to produce a representative set of verdicts that will assist the parties in reaching a global settlement. Permitting plaintiffs to dismiss cases on the eve of trial also can distort the information provided by bellwether trials.

Working together, courts can select the trials most likely to produce illustrative verdicts.

The representativeness of trials also can be diluted by jurisdictional differences in substantive law. It is important to keep in mind that the goal is to have bellwether trials that address the main points of contention between the parties. For example, joint and several liability rules vary by jurisdiction. A defendant that faces much greater potential liability in one jurisdiction than another will allocate its efforts accordingly. If the real battle is not being fought in your courtroom, consider deferring to the court where it is, provided that doing so will not compromise your case-management and case-disposition obligations and is consistent with your local rules and culture.

An effective approach is to divide related cases into categories, based on the key issues. The categories might be based on plaintiff characteristics, claim types, or applicable law. Select bellwethers from each category.

With all courts involved in multijurisdiction litigation working together, the trials selected can produce the most helpful verdicts while expending the least party and judicial resources.

Suggested reading

Eldon E. Fallon, Jeremy T. Grabill & Robert Pitard Wynne, *Bellwether Trials in Multidistrict Litigation*, 82 Tul. L. Rev. 2323 (2008)

Conclusion

Multijurisdiction litigation poses numerous challenges to the state and federal courts. With mutual respect and two-way communication, however, these challenges can be overcome. The key is to keep apprised of the progress of the litigation as a whole. Doing so will enable you to conserve resources, exploit efficiencies in discovery, and avoid one or more parties taking unfair advantage. In the end, successful coordination among multiple jurisdictions can lead to an efficient and fair resolution of the litigation.

Acknowledgments

The creation of this resource began with a resolution the Conference of Chief Justices (CCJ) adopted in January 2011. Because "multi-jurisdiction litigation, such as mass torts, can challenge the resources and ingenuity of both federal and state judiciaries" the CCJ called for "steps to promote communication between state and federal courts for the purpose of establishing best practices for the management of like-kind litigation that spans multiple state jurisdictions and federal districts."

This resource is based on the insights of a working group of ten judges—five state and five federal—with extensive experience in multijurisdiction litigation. A series of teleconferences and written exchanges culminated in a day-long conference in May 2012 addressing the challenges and opportunities involved in coordination. The project was a joint undertaking of the National Center for State Courts, the Judicial Panel on Multidistrict Litigation, and the Federal Judicial Center.

State-Federal Multijurisdiction Litigation Working Group:
Judge Charles R. Breyer (N.D. Cal.)
Justice Tracy Christopher (Tex. Ct. App.)
Judge Michael James Davis (D. Minn.)
Judge Carol E. Higbee (N.J. Super. Ct.)
Judge Sandra Mazer Moss (Pa. C.P. Ct.)
Judge J. Frederick Motz (D. Md.)
Judge Barbara J. Rothstein (W.D. Wash.)
Judge Cynthia M. Rufe (E.D. Pa.)
Judge Joseph L. Slights III (Del. Super. Ct.)
Judge Carl J. West (retired) (Cal. Super. Ct.)

The working group was supported by:
Judge Jeremy D. Fogel (Director, Federal Judicial Center)
Judge W. Royal Furgeson, Jr. (retired) (Judicial Panel on Multidistrict Litigation)
Judge Gregory E. Mize (National Center for State Courts)
Judge Richard W. Story (Committee on Federal–State Jurisdiction, Judicial Conference of the United States)

Appendix: General Resources

* Available for free download at www.ncsc.org
† Available for free download at www.fjc.gov

James G. Apple, Paula L. Hannaford, & G. Thomas Munsterman, Manual for Cooperation Between State and Federal Courts (Federal Judicial Center, National Center for State Courts, and State Justice Institute, 1997)* †

Michael Dore, *Reforming the New Jersey Supreme Court's Procedures for Consolidating Mass Tort Litigation: A Proposal for Disclosing the Rules of the Game*, 55 Rutgers L. Rev. 591 (2003)

Howard M. Erichson, *Informal Aggregation: Procedural and Ethical Implications of Coordination Among Counsel in Related Lawsuits*, 50 Duke L.J. 381 (2000)

Eldon E. Fallon, Jeremy T. Grabill & Robert Pitard Wynne, *Bellwether Trials in Multidistrict Litigation*, 82 Tul. L. Rev. 2323 (2008)

Federal Judicial Center, Manual for Complex Litigation, Fourth (2004)†

Hon. Helen E. Freedman, *Product Liability Issues in Mass Tort—View From the Bench*, 15 Touro L. Rev. 685 (1999)

Paula L. Hannaford-Agor, Comment: Federal MCL Fourth and Suggestions for State Court Management of Mass Litigation (National Center for State Courts 2006)*

Judicial Conference of the United States, Civil Litigation Management Manual (2d ed. 2010)†

Judicial Panel on Multidistrict Litigation & Federal Judicial Center, Ten Steps to Better Case Management: A Guide for Multidistrict Litigation Court Clerks (2008)†

Judicial Panel on Multidistrict Litigation & Federal Judicial Center, Ten Steps to Better Case Management: A Guide for Multidistrict Litigation Transferee Judges (2009)†

Francis E. McGovern, *An Analysis of Mass Torts for Judges*, 73 Tex. L. Rev. 1821 (1995)

Francis E. McGovern, *Rethinking Cooperation Among Judges in Mass Tort Litigation*, 44 UCLA L. Rev. 1851 (1997)

Francis E. McGovern, *Toward a Cooperative Strategy for Federal and State Judges in Mass Torts Litigation*, 148 Penn. L. Rev. 1867 (2000)

Geoffrey P. Miller, *Overlapping Class Actions*, 71 N.Y.U. L. Rev. 514 (1996)

Gregory E. Mize & James Fletcher, Judicial Ethics Considerations When Managing Multi-jurisdiction Litigation (National Center for State Courts 2012)*

Sandra Mazer Moss, *Response to Judicial Federalism: A Proposal to Amend the Multidistrict Litigation Statute from a State Judge's Perspective*, 73 Tex. L. Rev. 1573 (1995)

Joseph J. Ortego, James W. Weller, & Aaron S. Halpern, *Multidistrict Litigation and the Coordination of Complex Litigation*, Toxic Law Reporter, Oct. 9, 2008, at 898

Yvette Ostoloza & Michelle Hartmann, *Overview of Multidistrict Litigation Rules at the State and Federal Level*, 26 Rev. Litig. 47 (2007)

Paul D. Rheingold, *Prospects for Managing Mass Tort Litigation in the State Courts*, 31 Seton Hall L. Rev. 910 (2001)

Hon. Jane R. Roth, *Coordination of Litigation in State and Federal Courts*, in Business Commercial Litigation in Federal Court 147 (Robert L. Haig, ed., 3d ed. 2011)

Barbara J. Rothstein & Catherine R. Borden, Managing Multidistrict Litigation in Products Liability Cases: A Pocket Guide for Transferee Judges (Federal Judicial Center & Judicial Panel on Multidistrict Litigation, 2011)†

Barbara J. Rothstein & Thomas E. Willging, Managing Class Action Litigation: A Pocket Guide for Judges (Federal Judicial Center 2010)†

William W Schwarzer et al., *Judicial Federalism in Action: Coordination of Litigation in State and Federal Courts*, 78 Va. L. Rev. 1689 (1992)

E. Norman Veasey, *A Response to Professor Francis E. McGovern's Paper Entitled Toward a Cooperative Strategy for Federal and State Judges in Mass Tort Litigation*, 148 U. Pa. L. Rev. 1897 (2000)

Mark C. Weber, *Forum Allocation in Toxic Tort Cases: Lessons From the Tobacco Litigation and Other Recent Developments*, 26 Wm. & Mary Envtl. L. & Pol'y Rev. 93 (2001)

www.ingramcontent.com/pod-product-compliance
Lightning Source LLC
Chambersburg PA
CBHW070311190526
45169CB00004B/1585